HENRY PURCELL
A Miscellany of Songs

FOR ONE / TWO VOICES AND PIANO

REALISED BY BENJAMIN BRITTEN

FABER *ff* MUSIC

© 1994 by Faber Music Ltd
First published in 1994 by Faber Music Ltd
3 Queen Square London WC1N 3AU
Music processed by Christopher Hinkins
Cover design by S & M Tucker
Printed in England by Halstan & Co Ltd
All rights reserved

ISBN 0 571 51474 X

PREFATORY NOTE

This volume brings together five previously unpublished realisations by Benjamin Britten of vocal music by Henry Purcell, all of which were originally prepared for particular singers with whom Britten worked.

Britten's keyboard realisations of Purcell's original figured bass lines are highly personal in style and always intended for pianoforte. With the single exception of Purcell's own tempo indication of 'very slow' at bar 58 in *When Myra sings*, all the indications of dynamics and tempi are Britten's own or editorial when enclosed in square brackets. As Britten and Pears memorably remarked in the preface to their first volumes of Purcell arrangements (published by Boosey & Hawkes in the 1940s): 'it has been the constant endeavour of the arranger to apply to these realisations something of that mixture of clarity, brilliance, tenderness and strangeness which shines out in all Purcell's music'.

1 The Knotting Song (Z. 371)

Words by Sir Charles Sedley (*Miscellaneous Works*, 1702).

First published in *Thesaurus Musicus. . . The third book. . .* Printed by J. Heptinstall for John Hudgebutt . . . London, 1695.

Britten's realisation, one of his earliest Purcell realisations, was first performed by Peter Pears (tenor) accompanied by Benjamin Britten (piano) at a recital at the Hotel Henry Perkins, Riverhead, New York, 19 November 1939. It was also included in the programme for what turned out to be their last public performance together at The Maltings, Snape, in September 1972.

2 O Solitude, my sweetest choice (Z. 406)

Words by Katherine Philips (*Poems*, 1667).

First published in *Comes Amoris; or the Companion of Love. Being a choice collection of the newest songs now in use. . .* Printed by Nat. Thompson for John Carr and Sam. Scott. . . London, 1687.

Britten's realisation was first performed by Pears and Britten at the Wigmore Hall, 11 March 1955.

3 Celemene, pray tell me (Z. 584)

Words by Thomas D'Urfey. The duet was included in Thomas Southerne's tragedy *Oroonoko*, first produced in London in November 1695. (Southerne acknowledged his indebtedness to Aphra Behn's novel for the plot.)

First published in *Deliciae Musicae. . . The fourth book. . .* Printed by J. Heptinstall for Henry Playford . . . London, 1696. In *Delicae Musicae* it appears as 'A Dialogue in Oroonoko, sung by the Boy and Girl'.

Britten's realisation was first performed by Joan Cross (soprano), Pears and Britten at the Cambridge Arts Theatre, 10 February 1946. It remained a feature of their joint recitals together until Miss Cross's retirement in the mid-1950s.

4 Dulcibella, whene'er I sue for a kiss (Z. 485)

Words by Anthony Henly.

First published in *The Gentleman's Journey. . .* October and November, 1694; subsequently it appeared in *Orpheus Britannicus*, London, 1698.

Britten's realisation was first performed by James Bowman (counter-tenor), John Shirley-Quirk (bass-baritone) and Britten at The Maltings, Snape, 26 June 1971.

5 When Myra sings (Z. 521)

Words by George Granville, Lord Lansdowne, 1693.

First published in *Deliciae Musicae. . . The second book. . .* London, 1695.

Britten's realisation was first performed by Pears, John Shirley-Quirk (bass-baritone) and Britten at The Maltings, Snape, 26 June 1971, as part of a concert that included the first performance of Britten's *Canticle IV: Journey of the Magi* Op. 86.

Philip Reed
Aldeburgh, February 1994

The Knotting Song

HENRY PURCELL
realised by Benjamin Britten

CHARLES SEDLEY

Phyl-lis with-out___ a frown___ or___ smile sat___ and knot-ted, and

knot-ted, and knot-ted, and knot-ted___ all the___ while.

while.

O Solitude
A Ground

KATHERINE PHILIPS

HENRY PURCELL
realised by Benjamin Britten

tu - mult and from noise, How ye my rest - - - - less thoughts de-

-light! O So - li - tude! O So - li - tude! my

sweet - - - - est, sweet - est choice. O

Hea - vens what con - tent____ is mine To see those trees which have ap-

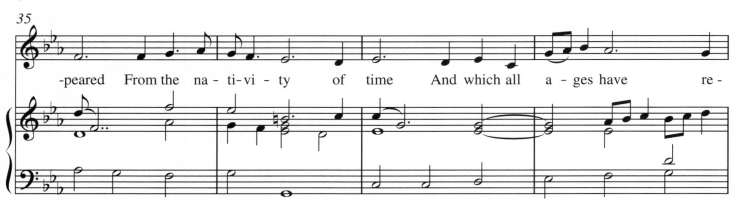

-peared From the na - ti - vi - ty of time And which all a - ges have re-

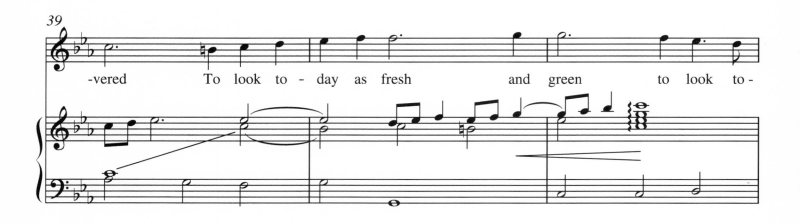

-vered To look to - day as fresh and green to look to-

-day as fresh and green As when their beau-ties first were

seen. O! O how a-

Celemene

A Dialogue in Oroonoko, sung by the Boy and Girl

THOMAS D'URFEY

HENRY PURCELL
realised by Benjamin Britten

ne -ver, pains__ I ne -ver, ne -ver, ne -ver felt be - fore.

And when thus__ I touch,_ when thus__ I touch_ your hand,

Why I wish,_ I wish,_ I wish__ I was__ a__ man?

Why I wish,_ I wish,_ I wish__ I was__ a__ man?

Dulcibella, whene'er I sue for a kiss

ANTHONY HENLEY

HENRY PURCELL
realised by Benjamin Britten

tell me, fair— one, tell— me why, You'll nei-ther let me live,———

tell— me, fair— one, tell— me why, You'll nei-ther let me

live,——— you'll nei-ther let me

nei-ther let me live——— nor——— die.

live——— nor die.

When Myra sings

GEORGE GRANVILLE

HENRY PURCELL
realised by Benjamin Britten

* grace-notes on the beat.

-ful as an - o - - ther's song?

-ful as an - o - - ther's song?

[Fast]

Such har - mo - ny, such wit, such har - mo - ny,

Such har - mo - ny, such wit, such

pp   *sim.*

such wit, such wit, a face___ so fair,

har - mo - ny, such wit, a face so fair,

So ma - ny, so ma - ny point - ed ar - rows who, who can bear?

So ma - ny, so ma - ny point - ed ar - rows who, who can bear?

The slave_ that from_ her wit,_ or beau - ty_ flies,

The slave that from her_ wit, or beau - ty flies,

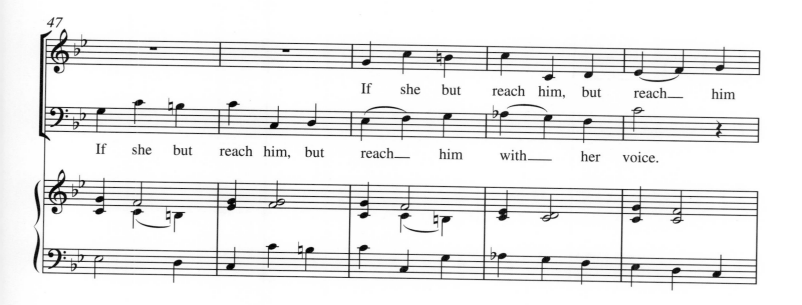

If she but reach him, but reach_ him

If she but reach him, but reach_ him with_ her voice.

slow arpegg.